NEW GHOSTS

New Ghosts

Laura Quinney

Borderland Books

Published by Borderland Books, Madison, WI
www.borderlandbooks.net

Publisher's Cataloging-In-Publication Data
Names: Quinney, Laura.
Title: New ghosts / Laura Quinney.
Description: First edition. | Madison, WI : Borderland Books, [2016]
Identifiers: LCCN 2016938010 | ISBN 978-0-9965052-5-3
Subjects: LCSH: American poetry—21st century.
Classification: LCC PS3617.U566 N49 2016 | DDC 811/.6—dc23

Printed in the United States of America
First edition

Contents

Slow

What I like
is to slow down
so much there is
almost absolute
silence almost
absolute stillness
as close at any rate
as a person
can get in this world

not meant for that
at all and rarely
to be found except
in some places
where there is quiet
water or a heap
of rocks upon rocks

in Rembrandt's painting
of the philosopher
he sits plainly
concentrating
but he is far away
in one dim corner while
an improbably large
spiral staircase rises
and twists through the dead
center of the room
whirling tornado-like
though it cannot move

what seems
to be turning
is still as a rock
and what is turning
is invisible
turning in itself
coiling
in its own way

in defiance
of everything
we know about life.

The Correct Answer

What is left
has to be stolen

it is part
of the world
and not
part of the world

made by human hands
perhaps
lighting up
human faces

but it has to be
snatched
and you
have to go apart
yourself
to know it

because it does not
sort with broad day

the clash and boom
snuffling and muttering

the flakes of ash
falling continually
in a dry rain

the watching

even in the midst of it
there is a form
of coming in
away from it

turning
to the blank side

where what counts
in the one world
as a dream
counts in the other
as the warming night.

Snowmelt, Midwinter

Drops falling from the eaves
with a steady satisfying beat
as if diving into the hard crust
of snow that wraps the yard
no matter to me sheltering
in my warm bed who have
dreamt so much already.

Themeless

Into the hollow of lyricism
and the swaying of verse
back and forth boustrephedon
like the ruffled gray water
in a tide pool I pour my love
of this unbespoken form
nothing in itself but motion
along the page and in the tongue
and mind plowing and turning
with the call of music alone
raising the mute what has been
required to be forgotten.

The Soul Is A Self-Moving Number

A self-humming
and a self-buzzing.

The hammer smashes.
The water floods.
The dove crosses
with its tickling,
expressive feet.

Some things adhere
like burrs on leaves
and leaves
on the windowpane.

Lazy Days of Summer

I tried thinking

but it failed

to lead me to

what I was

thinking about

and instead

I kept slipping

from one side

to the other

of my thought

like someone

trying to climb

the bare back

of an animal

so averse

was my thought

to being thought

by me

and I thought rather

of idle phrases

that would make

good titles

and of companionable

themes and of going

abroad to France

and of darker things

whose sting

has been worn down

by having been

thought before

and then

I came upon this

only another

sideways sliding

only half

answering

the purpose

because I know

what it feels like

a sharp

in a musical score

and what images

come with it

the old farm

the people there

and even so

these are

the safer images

for I cannot

get myself to go

from "of" to "that"

or think what lies

under the unbound

semblances.

Lighting Down

There are twelve or fourteen
house sparrows at the feeder
jostling for place or taking turns
while a few wait and watch
briefly on the roof of the garage
they are eating premium seed
meant for cardinals and blue jays
devouring an entire column
in a single day but the whirring
and flickering is worth the price
I lie on my bed watching them
reading *The Brothers Karamazov*
or *The Iliad* trying to read slowly
slowing down my breath to read
slowly since all this is for this
time that holds itself up
like a hand in its own shadow.

Reluctance

Our moods do not believe in each other.
— Emerson

Reluctance
to come in out of the mild

vacation of the spirit
to riffle

pull
and pluck on the old bones

leave them rather
lying in the hole

forever, or
until such time

as violence

sets them upright
and plants them

in the middle
of the road onward.

Control Option Command

Come to the age where there are
just words their beginnings
their combinations their turnings
their multi-colored shadows
like a cape they throw around them
come to this age with straight lines
the shortest distance no arcs
but a lull for music a chamber
of ambrosial differences
they are the total air
they do not need
to become anything the door is
thrown wide open but they
fill the hour completely
their time
is what the time was for.

Tree Pose

"Life is a bridge
from dream to dream"

not dream as in a wish
but dream as in illusion

one unsteady view
dissolving while another
swims together
to take its place

as the skipping stone
breaks one image
and skims onward
to the next until
the stone sinks

so when I was a girl
I survived by moving
and now
thanks to dreams I live
even by standing still.

Akimbo

It is good
to be a ghost

to drift
so lightly
through the world

that in the same way
it does without you
it has existed
only for you

and because
you leave a small gap
that soon fills in
you live here
as an observer might

curious

uncaught.

Feast

We ate what there was
in the larder and when
it was eaten up we went out
ranging in the night sniffing
the refuse thrust out of
the lips of garbage bins clawing
the Ziploc bags filled with wet
coffee grounds devouring the rinds
of who knows what rotten fruit
bolting the pith and the seeds
the bits of paper the aluminium
foil and Saran Wrap sticking
to them we ate the gristle and
the innards and the stripped-off skin
crackling the bones in our teeth
we tore at the crusts swallowed the pits
gnawed the Teflon slurped the mix
in the bottom of the bags
then we went home and lay in the yard
and we were still hungry.

Hunger and Thirst

I want to live
say most of the characters
in Chekhov's plays
and with a bang
!
it's a film (1958)
starring the starlet
Susan Hayward
as a woman framed
for murder threatened
with a sentence of death
and as a sentence
one of the great ones
whose meaning varies
with the age of the person
who says it
and is least complex
in the mouth of a dying man
because for him
it's obvious what it means
to live
but for the young
the older the oldest
still abiding it is what
they are still waiting for
the youngest can say
best what it is
everything

not here yet
later it is like
a fire of unknown origin
burning as we pass it
in the dark wood
condensing as it falls
farther and farther
backward in the night.

Synthetic Harbors

Not like the post you whip around
at the turning-point in the race
but slowly like the most
imperceptible curve that finds you
on the other side without
having noticed how
you got there when it was
you passed the point beginning
to flow down the other side
here we are watching
while the others live
gazing at some waiting for some
keeping the balance
as if we were the still ones
an island in the middle
of the freeway oh you jest
we are flowing down and we
know it and don't know it.

Progression Halo

One phase ends
   and another begins
and for a while
   they seem to climb
      upward like a flight of steps
then they turn and start
not so much
to cascade downward
as the metaphor implies
but to end
in a new way

to end
by really ending
   not pausing like a prelude
      but putting a stop to whatever
      kind of song was being sung
            and preparing in being sung
              to be sung some more
and saying:
that is all
that is all
   life passes through and on
backwards to another source.

Short-Circuit

However long
it takes
duration
has nonetheless
eluded its moment
look back
and it seems
the hill never
climbed
somehow
it stayed
low to the ground
though it appeared
on approach
to be a real crest
and to rise
under your
hastening feet
the slope didn't
manage to go
upwards
it was just
grassland
all the same
windswept
quiet
in spite of
thunderous noise

as we went "up"
and "up" and eventually
"down"
striving to claim
the imaginary summit.

Less Than All

It occurred to me
finally that the day
might not come

that the lifetime
of training and preparation
may be the whole
in itself and a person
can pass through the circuit
without completing it

the way a line
slopes upward
to the bar and swerves

asymptotically away
I went downstairs
in the night in my sleep
without knowing it
and woke in the dark
still rooms in the middle
of a dream that they were
bright and full of people.

New Ghosts

Many people
have lived in this house.
They have filled
its old wooden rooms
with their voices
and their footsteps
like sun
flooding in the window.

And you have been here
all this time seeing them
come and go.

When they arrive
it is marvelous.
You can eat dinner
together in the kitchen
with lamplight and radio.
You can read voyages
aloud and every day
you can watch ball games
whether it rains or not.

It is lovely but different
since it has all happened before
and you know they will leave
after a time and their faces
their voices their footfalls
will fill the house
with new ghosts.

Imaginary Friends

They are based on real people
on inciting smiles
and scraps of rapport
and an old Feng Shui
of good angles rising up
out of the past
in a sluice of sunlight
and they move around at ease
linger across the table
lounge in the armchairs
drift above the bed
wherever you are
when you speak to them
and they answer
we are first friends
as in the first times.

Confraternity of the Dry Tree

As it is
we live far apart
separated
as if forever
by miles of highway
running in all directions
coursing freely
on our behalf
who can go
almost nowhere

so we remain
joined by the sheerest
filaments
Ort clouds
transparent helices
floating as between
whole galaxies
in the one
distracted mind

and these ghosts
move in their dance
so slowly it is
infinitely slower
than the decisive
flame of things

jumping the breaks
lighting the forest crowns.

My Narrative Poem

In the underworld
in the Hall of Truth
before the thrones of
Isis and Osiris
and their sister
Nephthys and 42
lesser judges
the soul must
make its confession

swearing it has *not* done
a litany of wrongs

and its heart must be
weighed in the balance

if it is heavier
than an ostrich feather
it is burdened with crimes
and must be burnt
in the fire by the goddess
named for her task
She-Who-Devours-Evil-Hearts.

Evidently
the ancients
found it hard to credit
that anything
could be utterly
destroyed

only fire could do it

because everything
is plainly reconfigured
and recast and even
the dead are living
in their way

only fire
with its red-yellow-black
bodiless tossing
arching and springing
unpredictably
light-too-sure
heat-too-hot
cauterizing
in the crackle and silence
can do it.

To the Romans

First comes

the process of building

things up

and then

comes that of

taking them away

as a child is nursed

into a desire for life

and then shown

what living

entails

or as

a wave moves

by breaking

with a

resplendent crash

then slowly

gliding

up the sand

to level

whatever forms

it lay down last.

Footsteps

Until I looked
back I did not
know I had
already crossed
the strand
and had before
me the long
walk beside
the shore
going far out
into the distance
far as the eye
can see.

This is the shore
of the life
after life
the light
grey sky
always the same
the breeze
ruffling grass
in the dunes
the suck and
hollow
of the wave
the grey sky
the long strip

of water's edge
and the path
it makes
beside it.

Faux Debutant

The same thing
over and over
again in waves
and each time
the same shock
and the shock of
going under it
over and over.

The Killing at the Crossroads

Beneath the new phase

is the old one that had to die

though it was not old

it was young

and the new one

is old

tired

broken already

in the service of some

invisible refinement

but who for?

This is the large heap

from which you must

take and take

and if you should wish

to refuse

you are forbidden.

Take.

Loop After Loop

Silver wheels
are turning
and it comes
round as what
it was before
when it came
around to be
what it was
before that
each
revolution
seeming to turn
around in one
place one loop
but they are
somehow
invisibly
moving forward
loop after loop
spiraling ahead
so you wake up
way on down
way past
ferried by the straight
line hidden
in the coiling cycles.

Coursing

The things that get lost
go so easily

it is their nature

from the moment
they are born

they race
downhill to the open sea

the things we build up
take so much labor

they take so long
to grow little by little

even if they
spring up

the seed slept
for a thousand years

and they flicker
like pale grass in the sun

it is a huge effort
pushing the stone

at every reverse
we start up again

the slipping
and the gathering

the hole dug
the hole filled

not for substitution
not for compensation

not to wrest
gain out of loss

but from want

for what else
though it is not
repair

it is simply
taking the tools
in hand and beginning

some other thing
in some other place

necessity
wearing the mask of will.

A Single Anapest

Nay, truly, it was but yesterday.
Great cumulous clouds
blew up in a nimble wind
and the landscape swept forward
cleanly diagonal as in a view
of Haarlem with its bleaching grounds.
Everything was brisk indeed.
But when night came
it was late it had already
been the night for some time
when we found the still air and the stones
laid in the darkness long before
there and it was time to begin.

Snow Day

Terrible and beautiful
day out of the calendar
in which night follows
hard upon dawn
like a book that has lost
all its pages and thus
comes as a surprise
to the one who cradles it
some ends are foreseen
but arrive too soon while
others are both undreamt-of
and premature anything
that happens happens
before it should each kind
is a marvel but stealth
has much to recommend it
where the map said ocean
I found moonscape bowl
upon bowl of shadows.

Café des Abattoirs

So clever the astounding
surprises no one more
masterful no landscape
more irrational
upended volcano
ice cap in the glen
sand resting on the surface
of the lake these senseless
transfigurations
that never end never

Sans Everything

I start to see it—
the sheddings
and the whittlings
the depositions
the devoilations
the strippings
voluntary and
involuntary
of functions things
thoughts persons

what cannot be done anymore
dreamed anymore seen anymore
thought anymore

the house the friend the job
the view the legs the book
the wife the hands the tree
the night the air the mind

to each one coming of age
less all the time
periodically
systematically
as in a strict experiment

as if someone were curious.

The End of an Era

It was plain to see
marked on the calendar
decades in advance
incised on the future
as if the future
were a carvable thing
and I saw it with my own
blind eyes
thinking I knew it
and I did not.

Blind Passage

rounding the curve
without seeing it …
suddenly it is
behind you the landscape
has changed summer
into fall and you have brought
nothing with you
to survive on

Metamorphosis

It did not.

Like a school
of fish swimming
up to the surface
of the water to be fed
other phrases
have gathered round
this one nibbling at it
as if to devour what
it means it might
have been it might be
it was almost it was
always almost it has been
in my mind it is so
in imagination all these
cues putting up
a most valiant resistance
to what once was
fluid indeed able to take
what form it might
in theory but over
decades of blind
meandering unbeknownst
to me and before my
very eyes has hardened
into this lump of truth.

The Sixth Act

it was very still
where we came
after the tumults

and the great
thrashings in the trees
had died down

the winds that bellowed
like a beast in rage
tossings in the surf

then it cut
and all was very still

we lay quietly
as if seeking to attract
no further notice

like prey
who want to show
nothing is living here

don't see us
don't devour us

and in that hollow
we knew certainly
all we meant
was to survive

in the abstract
without tension
like the unstrung bow

because something
waiting in us
had to stop

waiting

Transition

As if it were a room
in the Quaker style
white walls plain wooden
floors slender blue
windows and a few
straight-backed chairs
no adornments
spare geometry
and in it a kind of light
flows the sun past its full
but not dusky just clear
light without light
stopping to show
hovering
in the empty room
for there is nobody
here but this
is to be my home.

What Of The Hands?

After having made
many arrangements
over the years
forging alliances
building up
a series of
fortifications
a town a city
a whole
civilization
with labor and pains
at the cost of a lifetime
in order to forestall
just this
and therefore
not expecting it
at some place
in the road
you must stop
and go on alone

remembering
images of yourself
as a child
as a girl
as a woman
a mother with her child
with tall children

how unlikely
a preparation
it seems now
how strange a way
to get here
to the snow-bound
forest.

Flirting with Surrender

In the painting
rough with greenery
masses of shrubs
leafy trees and trailing ivy
Italian sun rakes
across the white stone
figures in the empty garden
one woman in stone
in her flowing drapery
with an arm raised turns
away pivoting on one foot
only her back
in the falling drapery
and her hair and one side
of her cheek can be seen
we might turn away
like her since really
by now it is enough
and something in the air
has always said dissolve
blend fall into the growing
of the things that grow here
and who would care
now in particular
but something also says
no it wants to go on
to keep guessing
though it guesses

all to itself
though the making is a
desert sand let me go on

Descent

And they said Go into the forest
Bring back the multi-colored Bird
of Paradise and I went into the forest
searching for the exquisite Bird
of Paradise looking high and low
day after day fighting through the trees
curled up among the twigs and moss
at night until I grew too hungry
too weary to go on and I came back
home and they said Very well then
Go back to the forest seek the lovely
White Warbler and I went back
to the forest in search of the shy
White Warbler peering up and down
among the dense branches gently
shifting and sorting the leaves
in sun and shadow day after day
until I began to doubt and I turned back
to the village and they said All right
Go out again see if you can find
a dun-colored sparrow and I went
back into the heart of the forest
to find the common brown sparrow
I sat on the ground waiting and staring
among the insects sweating and stalking
day after day until I gave up hope
and slunk back and they said If nothing else
then make one make a bird out of clay

and leaves and sticks and I saw those things
in the dirt and built a clumsy bird out of clay
and leaves and sticks and carried it back
in the cradle of my hands
but by that time they were long gone.

Grande Galerie

In *Bande à Part* Anna Karina
and friends
run down the long hall
holding hands

and so have we
in the sped-up
version of our lives
which is time

racing
faster and faster
until the living
human forms become
slices of light
and fleet shadows

passing over the stares
the monitions
the adoring averted glances

of the permanent
woman and child
angel and lustrous man.

Four Things That Are the Same

The time of rising months
is very short.
The time of open years
is very short.
The time before the days
grow long is very short.
The time before the days
grow short is very short.

Stain in the Water

Now that my memory
is going I have started
to read narrative
histories containing
one huge block
after another of
trenchant details

details mainly of battles
since so much classic
history is the history
of warfare which when
only a small part
of what happened
to people was written down
monopolized attention

because it was the major event
again and again
erasing and redrawing
the world devouring
entire populations
the men killed
the women and children
sold into slavery
or slaughtered too

the assuagements
of civilization
arduously built up

in many layers
over time one step
slowly hauling itself
up over another
of a sudden smashed
and scattered as if gaily

reducing the great
cities and the minor cities
and the villages and the farmsteads
to burnt rubble
the birds coast through

Perinthus
Eretria
Carthage
Miletus
Lipara
Iasus
Plataea
Strongyle
Gophna
Antipatris
Jamnia
Scythopolis
Jerusalem

very little
remains to me
of their stories
as soon as I have read them

yet it is not nothing
almost no detail
it is true but a sense
at least of where
the detail ought to be

large blocks
not of blank white
but grey which when
looked at more closely
resolve into a hundred
thousand identical
pointillist dots signifying
the shadow of an atom
of forgotten information

the holding-place
of an experience
what I have read

and also
seen and heard
and said and felt
and what has
changing within me

as I proceed

white to grey
air to atmosphere
an emptiness to a
tinted vagueness

a stain in the water
to mark where time
moved over it

subtler
than we desire
but not after all

indiscernible.

Secret History

Where did this loss begin?
In the dream the sun
bleaches the mortar
of amalgamated cities,
and there I made a choice,
haphazardly,
because it did not seem
it could be the last.

Continually Too Late

His calamity is that he came into the world too early
and therefore continually comes too late.
—Kierkegaard

A difference in the
composition of sand
and soil a slight
irregularity a notch
over time becomes
the bend in the river

yielding to something
little by little
you become another
and one day uneasily
happen upon yourself.

Inertia

The one you think you are
stands still one foot forward
smiling the soft archaic smile
or it goes on and on as if
travelling a desert track
through the quiet world
into infinity
it is living long ago
knowing next to nothing
of the time in which you
find yourself and it cannot
learn on its own where you are
it has to be confounded
brought before those
who are as it used to be
the unformed who have
real smiles brighter than light
suddenly the difference
shows it what it is how far
from what it thought itself to be
deep in a land it does not
recognize stunned at its new
form flapping the strange cloak.

Clichés de Clichy

Delirious kingdom
in which I have failed
to live my life
I wolf you down.

Spare me,
clock-router,
hide me from earth.

I Still Have Two Selves and More

I still have two selves and more.

Once each dangled
fanciful wares before me
lush in their polar forms
though one was never true
it launched the game
the adventure and its
rich toothsome doubts.

Now that choice is
retrospective and I have
done what I did not know
I was bound to do
the one form reveals itself
in its own multitude
with all its small blind
forkings I failed to see
and I failed to follow
and from each rises
the ghost of a lost calling.

The Ready and Easy Way

I've come to like it
wisdom or laziness
whatever
let time itself
be the dream we rest on
a small thing
losing its contours
like the shape beneath the water
within the glade
within the forest or the cave
where we wandered
in the company of the sylphs
it was already an enchantment
and a trance no less
than this one and so why
does it seem to have been
a sort of truth it were
shame to have abandoned
or a gift that draws its meaning
from itself and to be easy now
in oblivion is a disgrace
a breach of faith
from change unwilled
unsought incomplete
and still speaking you should have
lived forever in the first trance
it was yours
it was the first.

The Unlived Life

The life
I failed to live
is still with me

following
at a distance

moving with me
like a light
in the woods
and pausing
sometimes
—both of us
motionless—
shining straight
into my eyes

then the trees
creak
the wind shifts
we move on

I do not know
what to do
with this light

shall I put it out

or does it serve
a purpose
with its solitary beam

what would I lose
never
seeing it again

nothing
one might say
yet I cannot
betray it twice

I am still
alive in it
though it was
never born

it is the truth
unsquandered

haunting the woods
floating
among the dark tree trunks.

Up From Under

The dream comes back
and I am now three lives
away from it
I have dreamt it
so many years
when it arrives I nod
there you are
still so full
of unfulfillment
still cresting
still breaking
though the realm of that
desire is so long gone
like a dream itself
I am glad to see you.